stones
in my
pocket

Also by Thisbe Lloyd:

Liver & onions,
Red wine & tears
heartsongs for the non-conformist

stones
in my
pocket

Thisbe Lloyd
co-photography Elizabeth Turfrey

Copyright © Thisbe Lloyd, 2019
Back cover image © Elizabeth Turfrey

The right of Thisbe Lloyd to be identified as the author of
this work has been asserted by her in accordance with
the Copyright, Designs and Patent Act 1988

Printed by Lightning Source

All rights reserved. No part of this publication may be reproduced,
distributed or transmitted in any form or by any means, electronic or
mechanical, without the express written permission of the publisher.

To the ones who truly see 'me', it's all I've ever asked.
"Allez les bleus"

and to my patient prince. Unwavering.

Contents

hear me	13
Fur Coat, No Knickers	17
barefooted girl	19
70s throwback	21
Table for One	23
soul sailors	25
circus act	27
black dog	29
15 Minutes of Fame	31
syntax error	33
the fall	35
stars of the small screen	37
smile for the camera	39
nan	41
catching fireflies	43
gone ghost	45
winged soul	47
one with nature	49
lay me down	51
i used to be someone	53
I'm Forever Blowing Bubbles	55
boudicca	59
voyager	61
lifejacket	65
gordian knot	67
Mission Accomplished	69
Love is Not	71
Serpent's Kiss	73
Don't Tell Mother	75
weather forecast	77
Queen of Fucking Everything	79
here be dragons	81
central reservation	83
the artisan	87
where's your head at?	91
release	93
rush of air	95
exchange rate	97
Heartbreak	99
Vulnerable adult	101
pan	103
the compassionless	105
Knee-high Socks	107
worthless silence	109
sleight of hand	111
ten storeys high	115
Forum	117
iron oxide	119
honour	121
william john	123
Red Snapper	125
nightlight	127
cartography	129
Vicarious Lunacy	131
Special Delivery	133
Oracle	135
$e=mc^2$	137
anchor	139
lights out	141
Depth of Field	147
mute button	149
stripped	151
hoist the sails	153
Ski Sunday	155

by my side	157	Monochrome	193
tumble turns	159	Arson	195
Set Piece	161	white horses	197
Hole	163	Don't Feed the Animals	199
Marmalade sandwiches	165	Status Update	203
shine	167	Bombshell	211
Medusa	169	sunken ships	213
Father's Day	171	fight or flight	215
arrival	173	look to the dawn	217
arizona	179	stay with me	219
fire	181	All Strings Attached	221
magnets	183	midnight caller	225
the emperor's new coat	185	Painting in a gallery	227
look to the sea	187	born wild	231
early closing	189	orion's belt	233
done	191	Sign Off	235

Foreword

Writing has always been a part of me. I didn't realise quite how much until my mum passed away and my mental health needed an avenue to escape down when it all felt too much. I kept my writing a secret between me, myself and I for a number of years. I'm not exactly sure what I was afraid of but it felt so very personal that it would have been akin to shaving off slices of me, presenting these to others on a plate to be deemed fit to eat, or destined for the bin.

Dealing with the challenges of being an emotional (over) thinker is to walk the undulating landscapes of Cumbria. Being aware of your environment may be part and parcel of the journey. However, the real challenge comes in trusting your own surefootedness and striding out on your own path. The ground shifts constantly and you notice each and every rock, tree root or pothole. I've broken many bones, metaphorically, along the way, but the scars heal and become part of who I am.

With the publication of my first book 'Liver and Onions. Red Wine and Tears', I managed to take a step into scary territory. My poetry is not written as a highly secret code which enables others to unscramble 'me'. Writing for me has always been a way of unscrambling the static in my own head, to release every emotion, good or bad. It acts as a check against what I think I feel and what I do feel. Sometimes the two match up; sometimes not. Sometimes what comes out allows me to reflect on the words on the page and realise the disparity in feeling and situation.

'Stones in my pockets' is a collection of portraits. The poems have been formed by various people, combinations of people and moments of elation and madness. As I say, they are not a

semaphore message for my life, but echoes of encounters and deep feelings which forced their way out through a keyboard. The photographs are deliberately harsh: the false masks of social media, the frustration of feeling unheard, the liberation of finding a voice, are all present in the images.

The concepts came from my desire to embrace the internal wrangling of my emotions; to somehow capture, visually, the visceral experience of being who I am. It is with great thanks to my wonderful friend Elizabeth Turfrey that I was able to. Her care and attention to detail enabled me to bring the ideas in my head to the camera lens. With her help and a few large gins, the shots came to life and found their way into this book. Also to my editor and designer, but above all much-valued friend, Rich Bray, for his time and patience.

Writing this book is a 'coming out' for me as a writer, a way of finding my voice and style.

This book is offered with thanks to my oak whose roots stand the firmest I have known; to my children who bring inspiration each and every day; and to my grandad, Bill Lloyd, who not only gave me my pen name, but also a love of words, music and an inherited ability to string short sentences together in a reasonable way. Also, to my mum who forged the woman I am today; to my stalwart friends who don't abandon me when I lose my mind; and finally, to each and every person who has made me feel something. You have crafted these pages, for which I am grateful.

To anyone caged by themselves, in thought processes, or lack of self-worth - write.

Do not write for anyone but yourself and be true '... for they will not liberate you until you let them go.'

hear me

sometimes, i talk
too much.

perhaps that
is my downfall.

sometimes, no one
listens.

perhaps that
is theirs.

Fur Coat, No Knickers

Mythical charms weaved.
Smoke and mirrors,
Gilded with Kaa's smile.
Husks of words
Trip from your tongue,
Spilling out from your silo,
Fermenting your followers.

You deal in disparaging whispers,
Desperate to retain your throne.
Duplicitous and snide,
Shape shifting, wannabe siren,
Perfecting performance to the crowd.

Critics review:
"Amateur and unconvincing".

barefooted girl

a tangled line of frayed twine,
wrapped and coiled,
around her hands.
away in distant lands,
her mind runs, and feet stumble.
remain and gain ground,
soft sounds,
feathers, dancing in the wind.

ink wash blues, stretch on.
poplars' tall figures,
sketched, on the horizon.
far beyond reach,
of whispers and lies,
of false surprise,
noise and confines
of social commentators.

she is free, to be.

70s throwback

black thick wool,
scratchy, in the way
only old clothes could be.
yet, still it brought comfort.
even as salty droplets
traced their wandering path,
across the relief of her face.
mind stretched, its finger tips,
drawing back the drapes,
hung heavy, on the past.

the rocking motion of the car,
street lights, casting their halos,
through her closed lids.
she breathed deep,
inhaling memories
as if camphor;
anaesthetic for the present,
the here and now.
ghosts held,
all but for a moment,
passing through smoke rings
of time, catching in her throat.

Table for One

Penne syntax, al dente.
Hollow meaning encased within,
Leaving the diner, unfulfilled.
Yet the server is ordained,
5 stars on the door,
Self-appointed,
To bolster their own cause.

The usual clientele note, not,
The validity of the claim.
They care not, for truths,
As they are force fed
Course after course,
Shallow bowls of fodder.
Topped with faux,
Middle class, froth.

And all of this, presented,
Served up,
With the finest available,
Lip service.

soul sailors

stretched out on the hull,
sails rise above,
reaching out to the midnight sky.
she sees in his eyes
infinite worlds,
where love collides.
meteor storms,
clearing their course.
the travellers' gazes extend,
beyond horizons,
to hidden shores,
reached only by hearts.
navigation, by the soul.

circus act

slender arch finds taut cable,
stepping out to the void.
don't look down,
or hesitate,
or falter.

fine line, tight rope.
end, out of sight, in the mist.
unbalanced centre,
core lost,
weakened mind.

trepid extensions, curled digits
tightening their grip below.
lifted head,
stance, tall.
bolstered heart.

only just coping,
but it's better than not.

black dog

not what you think,
or even expect.
there was a time
when your shape slept in shadow,
slipping in and out,
between blinked lids.

but now you creep,
slipper souled,
noiseless, unwelcome.
get behind me dark hound!
leashed, kennelled,
brought to heal.

for now, another,
cast in your mould
and yet, ever different,
silently stands by my side.
between you and i,
holding her ground.

weightless air
of simple acceptance.
cushioned treads,
stamp gently upon my heart.
head, high, free to new winds,
sending their path, my way.

15 Minutes of Fame

Your wish is simple and unwavering;
The bright lights of external verification,
Validation, appreciation, adoration.

Marionettes all dance to your tune;
Piped lift musak, unsophisticated,
Unimaginative, uneducated, unoriginal.

Mirror! Mirror!

Give us your answer do.

syntax error

ill-fitting words try to define
the substance of love.
well-meaning bards falter,
in eloquence,
stumble, in phrasing.

so, who am i, to try
and pin down,
capture,
nail,
ensnare,
such a will-o'-the-wisp?

an impossible quest.
for love is not for catching,
to be tied down,
by Lilliputians
such as me.
save to say,

it's just something about you.

the fall

he walks in to my world
unexpected and quietly.
breathes life to my soul,
catching my heart by surprise.
unprepared was i, for such a deep fall.
not down, but up,
to reach blue skies,
tumbling in to his eyes, his arms,
soaring with new wings.
lock keeper of my deepest chambers;
he is the key, the spark, the fire,
i know will last forever more.

stars of the small screen

big screen wonders
reflect in her eyes,
but small screen wonders
play out in her heart.
of time, just time,
where they can just be,
hero and heroine,
held by each other

ordinary, becomes extraordinary,
through their closeness.
no need for grand gestures.
for the simplest of acts
become magical,
when performed,
from deep within
a true love.

smile for the camera

when they come, their shadows creep
through the charged mass of wires.
sudden electrical storms,
tearing, at the calm.
strange visions, dance and sway,
clawed fingers, ripping out connections.

every ounce of strength used to recall
that place, deep down,
obscured from view.
exhausted, being me for the crowds.
spectacles, on reality, rationality,
fallen, from their chain.

pinhole, brownie box image,
inverted, blurred edges, misted lens.
shadows, deepen in contrast,
sliding scale of resilience.
aperture widening, desperately seeking
the lightning strikes, caught in the dark.

nan

custard jugs; willow pattern plates;
caravanettes; the smell of lavender;
sitting on walls will give you piles.

square-cut sausage meat; writing desk;
soft skin; don't bite your nails;
if i were 10 years younger.

ivory cross; the evil eye;
smartly dressed; german wine;
duck-egg blue and lilac purple.

long-handled hairbrush; tubigrips on knees;
toast on open fires; sugar in an egg cup;
birdbath in the garden.

coty l'aimant: i believe in fairies
red thermos; soft blankets
chicken drumsticks on picnics.

pink wicker chair; mrs pope;
salmon pub; stagecoach;
pineapple juice, sip don't guzzle.

i was the seventh child
of a seventh child.
remember me this way.

catching fireflies

who knows what makes the brilliant sparks
fly, up from deep within,
when you're near to me.

but, fly they do, and red embers burn,
fiery puppeteers,
lifting my smile.

i fumble to explain, the unexplainable,
with insufficient words.
must just be something

about

you.

gone ghost

and all at once
she felt the calm
of alone,
with herself.
she was disappeared.
invisible by anonymity.
striding through crowds,
in a jet stream, self-made.
face, embracing.
nostrils, flared,
breathing in deep.
eyes, engorged
with surrounding
existence.
no one saw,
as she simply,
went ghost.

winged soul

the glimmer of light
that flickered and danced,
from somewhere
just behind
the locked gate of her eyes,
fluttered, stuttered.
fleeting, fleeing
avoiding their grasp.
a winged, impish,
bundle of life force.

extinguished
by inconsistency,
expectation, projection,
harshness and scorn,
insecurities of others,
insecurities of herself.

ignited, once more,
by tenderness,
acceptance, understanding,
thought and care,
gentle challenge of others,
challenge of herself.

pulsing
its own, unique pathway,
navigation on a whim.
and in a trice,
gone.

one with nature

i hear the whisper of you
racing through the trees,
tossing my hair,
in the gentle way you do.
rushing, in to your jet stream,
eyes closed, mind open,
heart, billowing,
with a love, so strong.
i see the mirror of your eyes,
smiling in to mine.
in lakes and oceans,
flowing over my heart,
awash with you.
a love pure and true.

it is only you.

lay me down

as i slip on
the evening's slumbering
jacket of rest,
heart, mind, soul,
at peace.
thoughts drift to you,
as sleep lays down
its warming
blanket of dreams,
for to spend, just a while,
in the comfort of our universe.

i used to be someone

repeating patterns
of reinforced
spite.
no longer
do you look
in the mirror
and see who
we see.
born to
the wrong world,
not out
of place
in this.
synapses
alive
with wit
and knowledge.
overactive,
it's true,
but it's
who you are.
grieve, if you must,
for the man
we did not
know.
but now,
celebrate,
the man
we do.
he is someone.

I'm Forever Blowing Bubbles

A question of truth,
You stand tall
On your
Self-promoted
High ground.

When you talk,
How the bubbles
Fly, high.
Their rainbow skin
Distracts

From the truth.

BRANDED

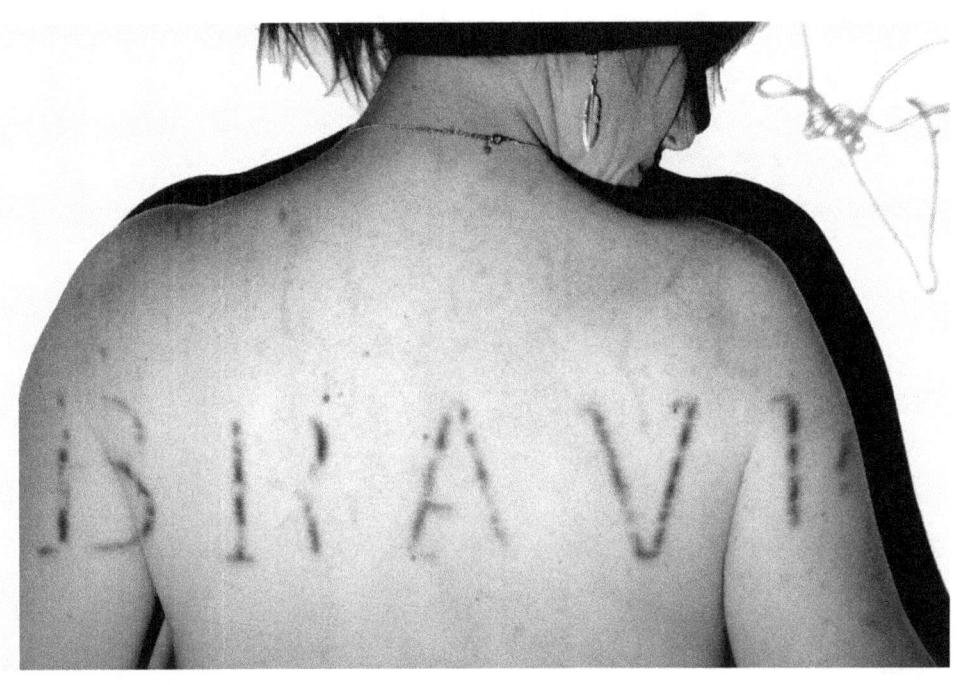

boudicca

and once the bleeding stopped,
tidal wave stemmed,
she looked upon herself.
bruised and beaten,
ripped to the core.
and then, creaking ribs stretched,
with the rise of her chest,
no longer with the ferocity,
of tiger's fight, teeth and claws.
muted stripe now ran through,
like Brighton rock.
yet, it brings no sugar rush;
no sweet, lingering taste.
foundations flawed,
she stands on stilts,
perilously close to being
washed away,
to the mercy of the sea.
the ebb and flow of life
stripping driftwood from her.

yet, she rises,
and so, she begins.

voyager

i am lost, in this
movement of time.
this world,
ever shifting beneath me.
wrenching my soul
from the safety of its cage.
trawled out,
for others to shame,
try to claim.
yet, it belongs to me.

as i fumble,
in the darkest of dark,
branches claw,
leave their marks.
pull me from my path,
to us.
scars, that
in time,
will heal,
with crumpled skin,
left, to gaze upon.

yet, you see me,
stripped bare,
standing there,
fight almost gone.
all at once, footings return.
scooped up,
in your arms,
sheltered from harm.
and for those moments,
i am found.

lifejacket

the darkest of the dark,
fight almost gone.
shutting down,
saving energy,
simply to stay afloat.
you slip around my shoulders,
tightest of fits,
and i can breathe,
once more.
buoyant, without effort.

your light,
from the shore,
whispers its call;
"save your fight,
i won't let you fall".

gordian knot

what to do when a soul's in love.
tenderised heart, battered thin
pressed, against its cage,
worn out and bleeding.

clipped wings beating; relentless.
redundant, without rising thermals
to lift it, to higher altitude, to soar
over white-tipped peaks.

what to do
when a soul's in love.

Mission Accomplished

Your battlecries slipped,
Through thin lips,
Falling on a widower's ear.
Sniffing out your prey
With a nose tuned
To loneliness,
And a shared desire
To please one's self.

Cast aside, cut out, disregard
Those, who make it hard
For you to win your prize.
Game plan in place,
Professional hustler
Deals her cards.
He chose not to see
Your sleight of hand.

Dealer wins.
Her house rules, only, apply.

Love is Not

Love is not something
To be touted around.
It is not something
That can just be written.
It is not something
That is a right, an inheritance;
Either by birth or association.
Love is not by proxy.

More than anything else
Love is an action.
Love does not need to be said
If it is shown, demonstrated.
Above all, love will
Rise above all obstacles.
It will not be stopped
By restrictions
You place, on others.

Serpent's Kiss

You talk of love, in your crass
Declarations, acclamations.
Implied, in your vacuous words,
Carefully crafted, dictation
And sent, with 'a loving kiss.'

But never cross the lioness
Or underestimate, anticipate
Her ferocity in defence of her cubs.
The snake may charm the young
But a mother's eye sees through.

Your dishonest smiles
Are not welcome here.

Don't Tell Mother

Conceited Traitor
Uncaring Witch
Nauseating Arrogance
Treacherous Tyrant

Tediously Calculating
Wicked Usurper
Abusively Needy
Toxic Trollop

Contemptable Troll
Uncompromising Whore
Noxious Aggressor
Tedious Tormentor

Threatening Coercive
Wantonly Unforgiving
Acridly Nefarious
Thoughtless Tramp

weather forecast

wild winds blow through this place,
echoes follow, whispering
their message, barely comprehensible.
dorothy would hitch up her skirts
and run, from the storms here.
the white rabbit, head first
down his hole,
would hurry to the queen,
or take tea with the hatter,
rather than dance, in this rain.

but, wild winds will never be tamed,
either by force, or coercion,
or false shame, decreed by edict of others.
they rage, they caress, they cut through
to where truth lies, all but hidden,
seeking willing travellers
of adventure and fire.
aladdin's entrance for those,
pure of heart, who can translate
the songs on these mistrals.

Queen of Fucking Everything

How satisfying for you,
On your throne,
Surveying your subjects.
But do not count me as one.
For you may choose to condone
Your own actions,
And justify your moralistic rule,
As bettering others' lives,
To yourself and your henchmen.
How easy it must seem,
Playing with fools,
Such as me.
Too stupid to read your moves
In the game, you play.

But I call 'bullshit'.

here be dragons

here on these pages,
i give you my songs.
set them free, from my mind.
allow them to burn
in the ether, all aglow.
wise words, said to me,
from a place of deep love,
'let them go, to the wind.
emancipate yourself from within.'
for they eat away, each day
overshadow my true melody,
'til a glance in the mirror
reflects back, clouded eyes,
vision over-exposed.
let these songs go!
listen hard for simple truths.
no second guesses.
forgive. forget.
take from these,
your lessons;
unclasp your hands
from words of bitterness.
for they will not liberate you
until
        you
                let
                        them
                              go.

central reservation

keep left of your line of sight,
steady your course.
one foot,
in front of the other,
on your meandering journey.
take in the view.
rubber-neck'ers
look on,
staring through you,
searching for the carnage.
road kill, laid bare.
the draw of the grey
pulls the eye,
pulls the head,
pulls the heart.
a different route to an end,
shorter,
quicker way to go.
but, stay left of your line of sight.
there's always
the hard shoulder.
pass on by
the central reservation.

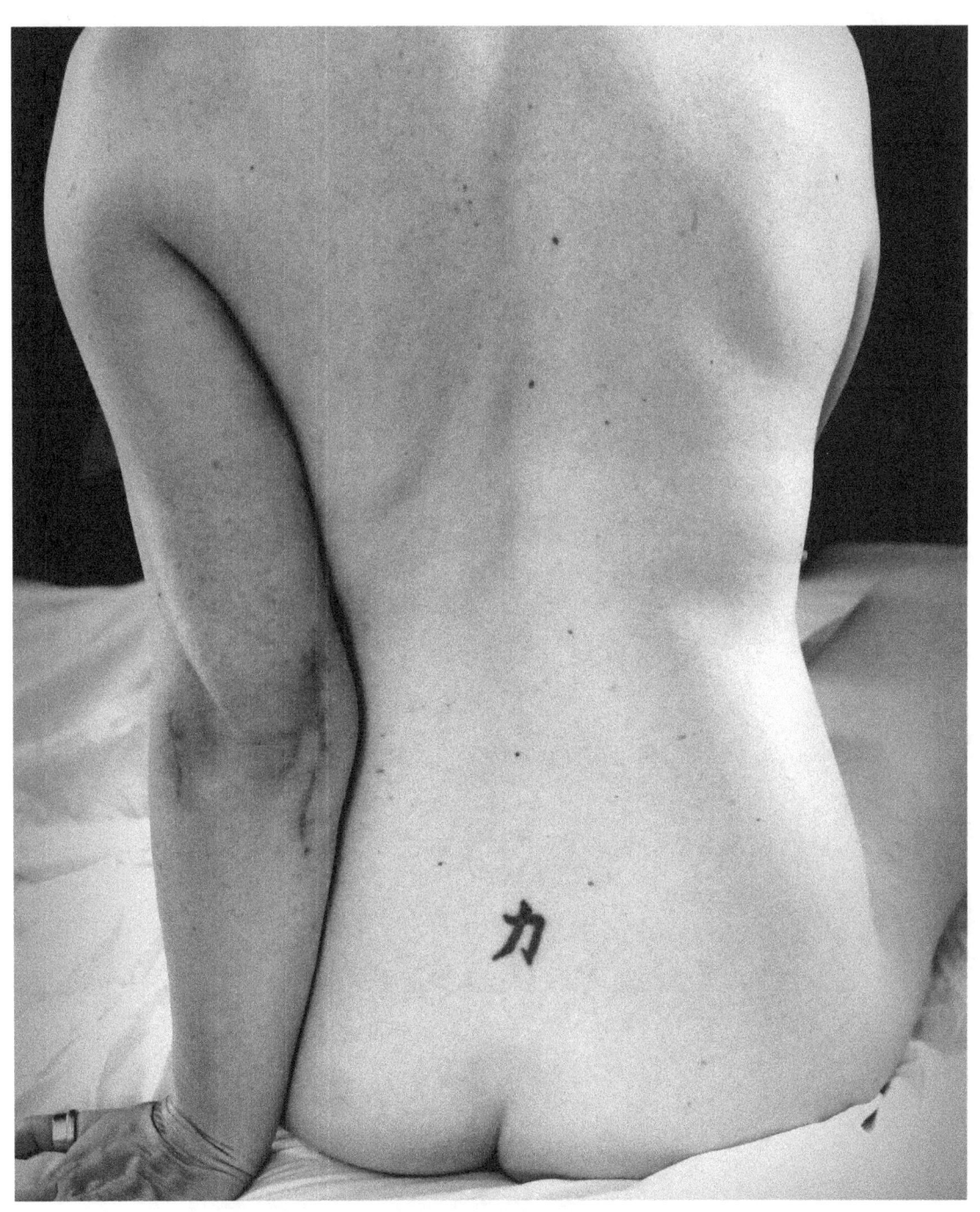

SCARRED PAST

the artisan

i carry stones,
in my pockets.
they gather,
with age.
when i was
young,
they wore
holes,
through the
fabric
and fell
silently,
unnoticed,
to the ground.
through
growing years,
like a beachcomber
of life,
each stone
left its mark.
some,
light as air,
defying
gravity's pull;
others,
stack,
in walls,
impervious.
history,
moves on,

graffiti
decorates
the perimeter,
testament to
its captive's
heart.
for i carry stones
in my pocket.

where's your head at?

lost, in the chambers of her head.
intrusive spirals,
frustratingly,
analytical,
nuances.
her ability to wrap thoughts,
so tightly,
around one thing,
it became vinyl
under her overthinking.
she sighed,
deep
as the darkest ocean,
slowly,
expelling
the breath.
it settled her,
refocused her,
reset the needle.
she closed her eyes,
saw the moment,
and placed pen to page.

release

my dear, she said,
there is no answer,
only what 'is'.
not bound,
in cotton wool,
nor assigned
to the madhouse.
she could ask for no more,
and she never did.

and, yet, it was given.

rush of air

she:
will you break my fall?
or catch me,
as i descend
from this height?

he:
i'll hold you tight.

just remember
to breathe.

exchange rate

it's been said,
more than once,
words carry power.
with your voice,
you may brandish
the sharpest of blades.
pick carefully
your weapons
of choice.
semantic shells
rain down,
ammunition of laymen,
without due care,
if blanks are fired.

all mouth, no trousers,
devalues the pound.

talk is cheap.

Heartbreak

You were supposed to be
There when I needed you.
Unconditional, so they say.
We propped you up,
Helped mend your heart.
Yet, you left us,
Without a glance back.
No man, nor woman
Ever broke my heart,
Except you.

Still, I love you.

Vulnerable adult

The inflection in your voice
Tells me you've soaked
In the medicine
You choose to self-prescribe.
Your timing, as ever,
Is less than perfect,
As I struggle to keep
My own head
Above the rising levels
Of work, children,
The wealth of
My own shit.

but, i see the child in you,
the desperate hope,
someone will see you.
it will not be him,
i assure you of that.
so, hold fast to the other side
where our strength
was built,
from solid foundations.
she never left you,
look within.
put down the bottle.

pan

there once lived a girl,
who never wanted
to grow up.

but she grew,
night and day.

the girl did not see,
changing times
of the years.

but she changed,
as she grew,
night and day.

now, the girl is a woman,
with heart, strong,
in her chest.

and she loved
as she changed,
as she grew,
night and day.

happily, ever after...?

the compassionless

acute anxiety,
in a room, full of people.
paralysed by noise,
by fear, by insecurity.

intrusive thoughts
thunder, in my head.
never-ending line
of mistakes made
at the command
of the dark clouds.

they don't forgive
the actions
of a scared soul.
with such torment,
raging on inside.

on my couch i lie
unable to leave the house
or bear to dress myself.
flashes upon my inward eye
the disappointed, judging faces
of the compassionless.

Knee-high Socks

You'll be fine,
Pull up those socks.
I mean, nothing
Really bad
Has happened to you.
Focus on the positives.
You're obsessed
With the negatives.
You're smiling,
In those photos,
On Facebook.
So, really?
You're feeling
A little low.
I mean, we all do,
At times.
You're not special.
You're so outspoken
And confident
I mean, what have
You
Got to be upset or
Depressed about?

worthless silence

what am i worth
if not to protect?
never, without reason,
or blind to truth.
but why will you
not speak?
time after time,
hammered down
with tongues.
scars left,
from lashes,
applied over years,
and no one spoke.
value established
from inactions
of others.
you wonder why
self-deprecation
and doubt
became
my stock position.

sleight of hand

do you see
who i see
when your gaze
falls upon
my face?
when i can't
raise my head
to meet my
own stare,
to observe
contour lines
falling across
features
i'd sooner change.
when the deep
pain of disappointment
rips apart
the strands
of who
i think i am.
you see mouth,
noise, laughs.
you see carefree,
no worries.
you see attention-seeker,
'look at me'.
perhaps, just perhaps
the person
you see
is a deflection.

just maybe,
i don't wish you
to actually
look
at
me.

ten storeys high

i stand,
looking down,
on the fall below.
toes to the edge,
but i'm scared
of heights.
you take my hand,
that smile
in your eyes.
feet first,
free-falling love.

Forum

Far seeing are you.
Knowing what's what
In my life.
Fuck you!
Your judgements
Carry no weight
In a real world
Of truth.
Appeal to the masses,
If you must.
Twist and craft
Your story.
It is not mine,
Nor theirs,
It never was.
Live life
On your box
Preaching
The good word
Of you.

iron oxide

when storm clouds come
and empty down their song,
drenched through, am i,
to the core of my bones.
for, no protection do i wear,
no armour of steel
to save me from such pain.
no summer's day warmth,
or tropical breeze,
could ever dry, completely,
this water-damaged soul.

honour

oh, weary prince,
with truest heart,
you wait, by my door,
ever patient, in hope.
tired, you must be,
of this lady's mind,
as, muddled and dark
it, so oft, can be.
and still, gallant one,
you hold fast, your steed.
no princess am i,
nor noble of heart.
you wait on a daughter
of damaged past.
she needs not, to be rescued,
but knows your quest
comes from the heart.

william john

more than you knew
i found myself, in you.
in the words,
that fill these pages,
the turn of phrase,
the pensive pen.
a closed book,
as a child.
stern exterior
masked a heart
and deepest soul.
your story burst
from the verses,
left, forgotten,
in old shoeboxes
and battered,
leather cases.
crammed to the edge
of the fag paper thin
rationed stationery,
your words
breathe new air.
we wasted such time.
i owe you a debt,
of these memories.
the smell of your cologne,
white vested shaver,
with inflatable biceps.
you left before
we finished our chats.

Red Snapper

Running scared
Of you.
Feels as if I have
Done so,
For a lifetime.
Floundering,
Slapping around
On the salty deck
Of my life,
Uncontrollably.
You leave me
Gasping for air,
Suffocating,
Under your control,
Observing my fight
To right myself.
A fish out of water,
Trying to ride
That bicycle.

nightlight

tracing over patterns,
weaved in to the fabric
of what makes me, me.
lost, as a child to rejection,
left to wonder,
who had my back?
no-one it would seem.
so, tears fell, silently
in to pillows, lit only
by a light that cast
dark shadows,
leaving marks,
deep in memories.
playlist, on repeat,
you wonder why
i move in anxious spirals.
the fight has been exhausting,
perhaps it's time, now, to rest.

cartography

parallel lines
of pathways,
crisscross,
conjoin
then part,
as forks
and spurs
are forged.
no maps
or compass.
no palms
to be read.
simply chance
happenings.
atlas of life.
tectonics, shift
continents,
tsunamis rage,
magma pours
revealing
igneous rocks
of fallen souls.

Vicarious Lunacy

I am not crazy,
Or stupid,
Or as daft
As you think
My gut tells me
Your lies are not
Made in my mind.

Don't place
Your guilt
And cowardice
On me.

Special Delivery

My gift to you
Is wrapped,
With a bow.
I've carefully
Packaged its contents.
Every item,
Labelled,
So you can tell,
What's what,
With ease.

You've tried,
Over years,
To transfer
Ownership, to me.
But, its rightfully
Yours.
Your shit.
Wrapped
With a bow
Of Fuck YOU.

Oracle

They live on hill,
Don't you know?
Observation towers
Built high.
Looking down
On the likes
Of you
And I.
Muttering
To themselves

$e=mc^2$

oh world, i am sick.
molecular'cholic
to my bones.
these electrons
pass through me,
interactions, jolting,
as strobe lighting,
jarring my senses.

oh world, i am sick.
the age-old dance
on illuminated floors,
stepping, in time
to the man
spinning the beats,
makes for dragging feet.

oh world, i am sick.
to my very core.
no longer do synapses
fire the wonders
of me.
the force is no longer
strong in this one.

anchor

sigh not, brave heart,
in despair, for she
loves e'er deep,
and strong.
though times
may seem, not so,
you are her,
and she,
you.

hold fast.

lights out

if tonight
brought the
last moment,
of me,
to you,
and all you had
left
was my
shadow;
what shapes
in the dark
hours
would be cast?
bold and emblazon
on your
mind's eye?
or, quiet
whispers
gently swaying
the willows?
shadows
will not cast
without
light.
and yours,
for me,
will
inevitably
go
out.

Depth of Field

The truth you see
Through your
Critical lens
Is false and untrue.
Focus your eyes
To the horizon,
Widen that depth
Of field.
The house of mirrors
Invites you in.
Will you see who
I am
For the masses?
For you?

Fragmented,
Yet whole.

Unpack the story
Of who I am.

mute button

slowly, she slips
in to the warmth
of oblivion.
her head
is silenced,
for once.
self-conversation,
volume on mute.
a stillness
unknown,
to her.
static,
removed.
how she longs
for the void.

stripped

am i, who you wish,
who you want,
who you long for?
perfection
is not who i am.
will this do?

hoist the sails

staring, between worlds,
where edges blur,
yet acuity sharpens.
endless time,
stretching out
its long fingers
of, 'yet to come'.
loosening her grip
on the old pier,
stepping, cautiously,
on to bobbing,
knotted slats,
catching the rise,
and fall, in a dance.
rope, thrown clear,
set adrift
in possibility.

Ski Sunday

Snow makes me sad.
Fumbling to grab
The telephone receiver,
Dial him up.
A smile down the line
His, and mine.
Shared game of speed,
Only with him.
The player withdraws.
Now with each fall
The line remains silent,
He is gone.

by my side

i know how i
can be,
all or nothing,
barely, in between.
and i know, when
i drop,
like a stone,
to below,
i'm a challenge.
so, you
carefully,
quietly,
patiently,
slide your heart
next to mine,
and let me hear
its beat.
through the static
it steadily drums
our song,
unfaltering.
i know how i
can be,
and i'm glad
you still came.

tumble turns

with deepest sighs
and through his eyes,
love falls and spills.
avalanche of heart,
right from the start.
engulfing her soul.

Set Piece

Pawn, in your set,
A means to an end.
Player's check-mate
And discard the waste.

But who are these
Pieces, pushed
To the side?

Heartless Queen,
Insecure, in her reign.
The King, merely
Follows suit.

Protection for none
But those, of use
And no threat.

New balls, please.

Hole

You seem
To be missing
That crucial part,
To be the person
I once knew.

Perhaps,
It was never there.

Marmalade sandwiches

Lift the rusted latches,
Tarnished and worn.
Soft leather, stained
And bruised.
Spill the contents
To the floor,
Vomit its spoils
In twisted piles.

Now, to unpick,
Sort and repack.
Funny, isn't it,
To look upon
The treasure.
Far from expectations
It will never
Fit in the same way.

Something, has changed.

shine

trust in yourself,
for you are my hope
for a soul that exists,
at ease with its shape.
a lightness within you,
a child, still at play.
yet, do not assume
this woman holds
no wisdom.

delight, in the
simplicity of a world,
seen, through
a carved lens.
splintering visions
of wonder,
of curiosity.

a heart so content
to, just be.
charming, engaging
accepting,
almost too large
for its frame,
its joy bursts
from your eyes.
calm in your chaos,
when i think of you,
i am restored.

Medusa

Who are you, really?
When all's stripped away.
Bare, standing, naked
In the cold light of day.

Nothing hidden from eyesight,
Pure, essence, of you
Will your myth stand inspection,
Or will truth, now, shine through?

Your mask slips and uncovers,
To those who know how to look,
Your delusions of grandeur,
They read, like a book.

So, play the persona
You've so carefully crafted
But be mindful of those
You have truly shafted.

Stepped on, and over,
Used to conquer your goal
Their hearts, you don't care for
But it damages your soul.

When you look in that mirror
You see what you choose
But look, slightly deeper;
It is you, who abuse.

Father's Day

Separation
Rips open
Her heart.

Execution;
By absence

arrival

hooded figure,
head, bowed,
shoulders follow.
emergence,
divergence,
from past
to now.
she is here.
she has arrived.

UNSHACKLED

arizona

flames lick
around her.
dancing silks,
flickering,
enveloping
her frame.
eyes fixed,
certain,
on the view.
from nowhere,
sparks
fuel
the heat.
magnificent wings,
unfolding,
beat down
as she rises.

fire

the winds blew
through, to her heart.
steeling herself,
she rose, from her bed.
no more would she
lay herself down
and be defeated.
sharpened, mind's eye.
focused, far.
she saw her destination
could be chosen,
by her.
no more afraid,
she reached out,
and took it
for herself.

magnets

dreaming dreams
of walking
hand in hand
with you
on distant shores
and well-trod
paths
familiar hills
tracing
memories
across
my heart.

always navigating
with the compass
of my soul.
north will always
find
you.

the emperor's new coat

heavy sheets
lie, across my body
holding
me hostage
to their density;
their darkness;
their suffocating
dark.

weighty cloth,
denying my skin, my mind,
what it is
to feel.
numbing threads,
blackout blinds.
the seamstress;
black bitch.

look to the sea

i will not fold
or crumble
or break.
the sun will
still rise
and there
will always
be music,
somewhere,
within this heart.

build some
walls
of courage,
with views
to the sea.
look to
the white horses
to calm,
and steel
this soul.

early closing

like a warm honey
dressing gown,
poured, head
to toe
tied, at the waist
with a 'fuck you'
bow.
lids, holding
lead weights
'early closing'
sign, turned,
silently conscious,
her jury's
adjourned.
heavy to the shoulders,
she can carry
no more.
her eyes tell the story,
her heart kept the
score.
sinking in velvet
grassy mattress
below
last whisper of life lust
takes its last bow.

done

lead weighted
from within.
every move
exhausts her.

Monochrome

Rain down your words
Of hate,
For they are
No more than
I deserve.

No matter how tight
I curl,
They slice open
My skin, my flesh
To the bone.

Your rage brings fire
To tongues,
Quick to burn
Their branding marks,
Soul deep.

Razor's edge of hostility
And loathing.
Love lost,
Beyond repair,
Or care.

Spit upon me your
Disgust,
But when your eyes
Open, you will see
All is not

Black & white.

Arson

Burn down your
House
Of bullshit &
Lies.

The glowing
Embers
Make for
Perfect
Celebration
Confetti.

white horses

sailing away on
waves, that bow
their heads, as if
to say, 'follow me'.
white froth
fingers reach out,
pulling the vessel,
gently nodding
its bow in agreement.
no wind.
no sound.
just calm,
lapping waters
send her on her way.
adventures, beyond
the horizon.

Don't Feed the Animals

No matter what
They tell you,
Or how
They beg,
Don't feed the Animals.

Their stomachs
Don't need lining
With scraps
From your heart.
Don't feed the Animals.

Parasitic are they,
In their
Take-Take world.
Diet of coercion.
Don't feed the Animals.

They will cry
For more food,
To satisfy
Their insecurities.
But, you must never
Feed the Animals.

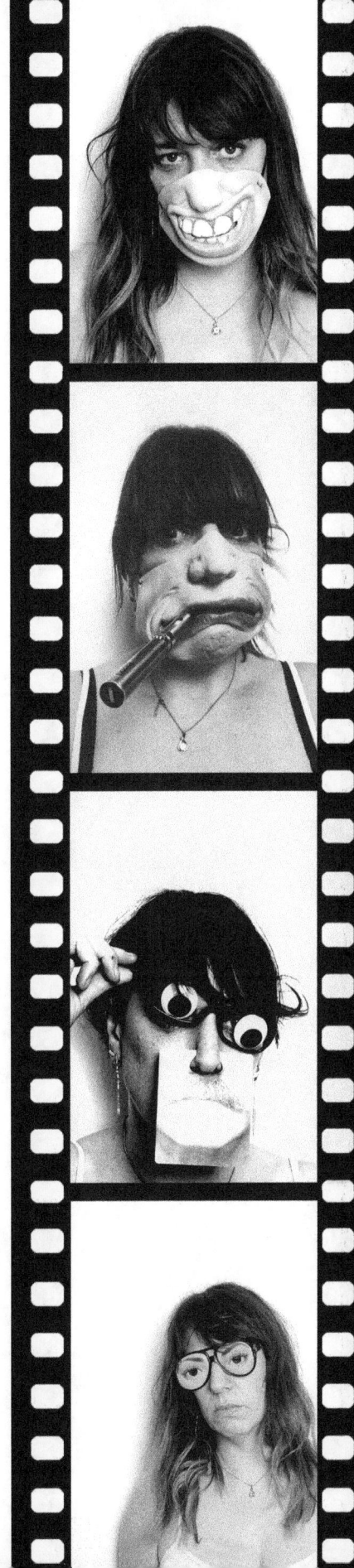

WHAT'S ON YOUR MIND?

Status Update

Where to start;
Is this the place
To spill my heart,
My thoughts,
My face?

Each profile pic
And status,
Filled
With tits and teeth,
Or sentiment,
Grilled
For explanation,
Grab attention,
Fun and frolics
And mostly
Bollocks.

Competition stage
For those with
Issues.
A public arena,
To dismiss you.
'Likes' carry meaning,
Public nods,
To demonstrate
Sycophants
Doing their job.

Thumbs up.
Love.
Sad face.
Dislike.
Social platform,
For open mic.

The darker side
Of public display,
Choice to
Ignore
Has much to say.
The game players;
Social slayers;
Fake and the needy,
Soak up the action,
Vanity greedy.

Judgement
On postings,
Everyday fodder,
For those
Chess playing
Strategists,
Narcissists,
Fantasists.
All two a penny
Choose your
Friends
Wisely,
It pays to have many.

External verification
Comes at a cost.
Life
Through a lens,
Lost
In the ether.

Disconnected reality.
Personality.
Who will you be?
A veneer of
Yourself,
Or chameleon
Shape shifter?

What you see,
On your screen,
Is not always me.
Why would I show
Where my mind
Takes my thoughts,
And I go
In to blackness?

Step back,
Take a look,
You feckless fool.
I choose
What I post,
As do you.

So, spare me
Ambiguous
Updates,
Tagging
Of best mates.
A mask we all wear,
Society's masquerade,
Through it
We wade.

I choose to decline,
Disengage.
You want me?
Then call me.

Let's do coffee.

Bombshell

Well, just look at you
With your coiffured hair
Fawning and faking
Your way through this world.

Howling battle cries
To your pack.
Circle your wagons
Against harmless foe.

Withhold kind words
For those who deserve
Gush your sycophantic
Emptiness only to allies.

You have nothing to say
And you say it too loudly.

sunken ships

bring back to me
the ember glow,
the roaring fire
from belly below.

be gone away,
caverns, all dark
drowning within
this numbness, so stark.

i'm, oh, so very tired

fight or flight

turmoil of
irrational tides,
endlessly battering
her fight.
she fears
her inadequacy
will make him flee.
hard to love,
in the depths
of her
faults.

look to the dawn

in her darkness
she sometimes
forgets
to look up
to the light.

the sun will
rise again
soon.

stay with me

your breath,
through my hair,
swaying the branches
of my dream's willows.
gentle fingers
trailing in the waters
of my mind's lakes.

All Strings Attached

I do not care for
Your passivity
In attack
Lego-headed turns
Of your
Multiple facets

Do you think
I don't see
Or fail to observe
Your underhand
Tactics
Of manipulation?

Blind, others, may be
To your snake-like
Charms
As your PR machine
Turns wheels
And heads.

Insipid pillow talk
Flows from
Those damning lips
Quick to project
Your own
Insecure anger.

Arse-covering
Self-publicist
You lead
Them all
A merry jig.
I care not for you.

midnight caller

i close my eyes
in midnight slumber
this is our
meeting place.
some nights
you come
others, not.
dawn breaks,
the night
and my heart
at times,
when you slip away
from my side.
adjustments of time,
hands always
marching, clockwise
onwards.
you left us behind.
one moment more
flies on
a million
dandelion wings.

Painting in a gallery

Where are the lines
Defining who we are?
I look to others
For guidance
Yet, their borders
Seek to keep me
Boxed.

Raging,
Passionate,
Joyous
Childish
Heart
Will not,
Can not,
Fit in keeping
With
Others' design.

They choose to read
A different story,
View an alternative
Work of art.

Shame on them,
Remaining
Blind,
To me.

What scares them
Weakens their
Character,
Not mine.

born wild

these whispers
of mist
could not touch, or
damage,
if she stood fast.

so, she chose
to stand,
and find her spark
inside.
to return to her
wild, wild heart.

orion's belt

bright stars
find strength
in constellations.
they burn
with a brilliance
that warms
the most distant planets
without
casting shadows.

Sign Off

... and,
in conclusion,
you are
both
a pair
of cunts.

Liver & onions, Red wine & tears
heartsongs for the non-conformist

Sometimes, if we listen carefully enough, we hear the forgotten songs of ourselves. In times of intense emotion, in loss, in despair, in love, lyric and score find their way to the page, take us by the hand and hold us upright when we most need it.

Liver and Onions, heartsongs for the non-conformist, is a collection of life's challenges, spilled out on to the page, expressed through a writer's need and wish to order a cluttered mind.

Unique to us, those songs are ours to claim, regardless of others' inability to understand when they appear disharmonious to an ear unwilling to listen.

Who's to say what dreams are made of?

www.ingramcontent.com/pod-product-compliance
Lightning Source LLC
Chambersburg PA
CBHW060505240426
43661CB00007B/928